Restoration
THE POWER OF THE BLOOD

Paula White

Scribe

Restoration: The Power of the Blood

Copyright © 2005 Paula White
Paula White Ministries
2511 Without Walls International Place
Tampa, FL 33607

Published by Scribe
4203 Elkins Avenue
Nashville, TN 37209

Written in cooperation with Dan DePriest of Scribe, Nashville, Tennessee
Cover and Interior Design by Sharon Collins of Artichoke Design, Nashville,
    Tennessee

All Scripture quotations in this book, unless otherwise indicated, are taken from
the Holy Bible King James Version.

ISBN: 0-9760-0662-6
Printed in the United States of America
06 07 08 CHG 5 4 3 2

Table of Contents

~ *Introduction* ~

Greater love hath no man than this, that a man lay down his life for his friends. Ye are my friends, if ye do whatsoever I command you. Henceforth I call you not servants; for the servant knoweth not what his lord doeth: but I have called you friends; for all things that I have heard of my Father I have made known unto you. Ye have not chosen me, but I have chosen you, and ordained you, that ye should go and bring forth fruit, and that your fruit should remain: that whatsoever ye shall ask of the Father in my name, he may give it you. These things I command you, that ye love one another.

~ *JOHN 15:13-17*

A Vietnam War medic tells the story of a life-changing experience he had during his tour of duty. He witnessed an act of great love and willing sacrifice by a seven-year-old Vietnamese orphan boy. The boy came forward when a matching blood donor was needed to help save the life of another boy who also happened to be his friend. As the medic began to perform the transfusion, the young volunteer began to cry. The medic tried to calm the boy, telling him that he didn't have to give his blood if he was afraid. But the boy cried, "Please, I want my friend to live!" So the medic continued. But the boy cried again. The medic tried to comfort the boy. "Don't be afraid," he said. "You're doing a kind thing for your friend." To his surprise, the boy asked, "When will I die?"

The medic struggles when he tries to describe how completely undone he was by the depth of the boy's love for his friend. You see, the boy believed he would have to give all his blood in order to save his friend. The medic was happy to correct the boy's misunderstanding and reassure him that they would both live to play together.

In the boy's face, the soldier could see a stark truth: He had never sacrificed anything out of love. From that day forward, he was less proud of his volunteer medical work and more thankful for it.

* * *

The shedding of blood by a loving seven-year-old boy had miracle-working power in the heart of a proud, tough-minded, battle-hardened soldier. But for two thousand years, the blood of Jesus Christ has worked miracles in millions of hearts. It has poured out healing to the sick and crippled. It has claimed victories in troubled lives, in difficult mission fields, for enslaved peoples, in prisons, and in entire families. It has forced open closed doors and closed nations. It has brought abundance back to dying fields. It has given restoration to cursed lands and repentant souls. The blood of Jesus has unstoppable power to convict and soften a hardened heart, uncover truth in the middle of lies, shield against works of evil, heal the sick and broken, deliver the oppressed, and even raise the dead. It is the loving sacrifice of blood that offers all this to us.

It offers so much more than we can comprehend.

Love that is greater and richer than any poet can describe is what gives the blood of Jesus its power to save souls, conquer evil, and heal a broken world. That love is the love of God. And the blood of Jesus is the only key that unlocks the door to God's powerful love.

Think for a moment. Do you desire healing? Do you want your children to live godly lives? How can you experience God's strength through difficult challenges? Do you want to be blessed so you can be a blessing to others? What can you do to help the world know Jesus better? If you want these things then you want the same things God wants. Today, a message of restoration is being revealed to you. And our great God is in the business of restoration—seeking and saving that which has been lost.

My friends, when you trust in the blood of Jesus as your only ransom from sin and eternal death, and you trust in Jesus as your only source of true life then you are in the center of God's love. And God is in the center of all things. Nothing exists which God doesn't own and have authority over, and He has given that authority to Jesus because Jesus shed His blood and claimed victory over death. When you claim the will of God over something in the authority and power of Jesus' blood, you bring God's will to bear upon the thing you are speaking over.

We shall see, however, that it is possible for you to speak the will of God, claim the blood of Jesus, and drink the cup of communion in an unworthy manner. And then there is no miracle because you have done a false thing. There may even be some level of discipline applied.

But before we look at how we can be true to the blood of Jesus, let's marvel together at a few of the wondrous mysteries about the blood and the wisdom of God's plan for our restoration.

~ *Part One* ~

THE SIGNIFICANCE
OF THE BLOOD

*O the depth of the riches both of the wisdom and
knowledge of God! how unsearchable are his
judgments, and his ways past finding out! For
who hath known the mind of the Lord? or who
hath been his counsellor? Or who hath first given
to him, and it shall be recompensed unto him
again? For of him, and through him, and to him,
are all things: to whom be glory for ever.*

~ROMANS 11:33-36

The word glory in this Scripture verse from
Romans is also translated "honor," "praise," or

"worship" in other parts of the Bible. And glory belongs to God forever because all things exist through God. He started everything; nothing was given to Him. And all things exist to Him—for His purposes and glory. God is holy. He is perfect in power, love, and purity. And everything He made was good because it revealed His holiness. All of creation, including man, was made holy because in all things, including us, God's holiness was to be seen.

The Bible says God formed man from the dust and breathed the breath of life into him. That breath of life wasn't just a divine CPR technique that jump-started Adam to life. God speaks things into existence. He could have formed man into a living, breathing creature from the ground up; but He chose to fill Adam with His life. Despite our intelligence and willingness to learn, the truth is that we will never be able to fully understand what the image of God truly is. Throughout eternity, there will always be something new about God to discover that will astonish us.

But something of God's own image and

essence was put into Adam so he could know God intimately—in a way no other creature could. Apparently, God wanted to be known and understood on a level that even the angels couldn't know Him. I believe the story of creation gives us a clue into what was in God's heart when He made Man.

⌐ ADAM AND EVE ¬

Remember that God brought all the animals to Adam to see what he would call them (Genesis 2:19). Naming the animals was a good way for Adam to start acting out the dominion God had given him. But he was also relating to his dominion. Naming the animals was an authoritative act; but it was also a way of describing how he knew them. In the process, Adam found that he could understand the animals far better than they could understand him. Even the most intelligent, warm-blooded animals were not like him enough to truly know him. Adam was the prince over a glorious earth. But he was alone; and God said it isn't good for man to be alone.

God wanted Adam to understand intimate relationship. He wanted Adam to see that he could only be truly known by another creature like him. Once again, God is so powerful He could have formed a mate out of the dust from which He made Adam; but He chose to give Adam a mate that was more than just like him. God borrowed something from Adam to form Eve so that she would be partly of him. God didn't breathe life into Eve; the rib taken from Adam had God's life in it. He wanted her life to come from Him through Adam. That rib wasn't dry, dead bone. It was living tissue with the blood of life in it. It is no coincidence, then, that our bone marrow is necessary for life-sustaining blood production. It's alive! And when God brought Eve to Adam, Adam's response shows that he understood the significant difference between her and all other creatures. He said, "This is now bone of my bones, and flesh of my flesh: she shall be called Woman, because she was taken out of Man" (Genesis 2:23).

Eve was created in the image of God just as much as Adam. It was the life-giving breath of

God in Adam's blood that gave life to Eve.

But the breath of God is also spiritual life that makes it possible to know Him more intimately. As long as God's life flowed inside Adam and Eve, they would live and know God intimately and forever. They were made to be something like Him and even partly of Him. In other words, God created Man in His own image and breathed His own life into him so that the whole family of Man would be more than just the most sophisticated part of His creation. God wanted Man to know Him and understand His heart on a level that was only possible because God gave Man a part of Himself. That doesn't mean Adam could have ever fully understood God or could have been completely like God. But God did put something of Himself into Adam just as part of Adam was used to make Eve.

To avoid any misunderstanding, don't mistake this teaching for pagan ideas of God being in all things or all things being God, for no human will ever evolve into who and what God is. The Bible is very clear on this point. God created space, time, the heavens, the earth, and all creatures as completely separate things from Himself. But the Bible is almost as clear to explain that God created everything so He could reveal Himself in a special way to one part of His creation. He desires a deep relationship with us. The Bible tells us that the deep level of trusting intimacy God desires with Man is best symbolized by marriage. Isaiah 54:5 says, "For thy Maker is thine husband; the Lord of hosts is his name; and thy Redeemer the Holy One of Israel." Look at Matthew 19:4-6 in your Bible. It says God "made them male and female, And said, For this cause shall a man leave father and mother, and shall cleave to his wife; and they twain shall be one flesh…"

⌐ A FAMILY HERITAGE ¬

The angels are called "sons of God" in the Bible; but they weren't created in His image. They were, however, created to worship Him and reflect His holiness. The image of God is a subject too great for this book so we won't go deeply into it here. Suffice it to say, God gave Adam special anointing and purpose that allowed him to be intimate with God in a way nothing else ever would.

Adam was then commanded to multiply and fill the earth with family that would inherit that blessing of intimate relationship with God. They would be living testimonies that God is in the center of it all. These blessings would be a family heritage for all time. Of course, all creation is precious to God. All creation is "of Him, and through Him, and to Him." But God's relationship with Adam was more personal—the way a father is closer with his son than he is with someone else, like the mailman or the grocery store manager. The importance of this teaching is that Adam's entire bloodline (including Eve) carries this image. And we know a large part of this image was hurt or lost by the fall when Adam sinned. We know, without being born again, no one can even approach God, let alone know Him or be intimate with Him. Without being born again, no one can see (have "revelation-understanding of") the kingdom of heaven, which we'll examine in a later section.

⌐ Satan's Envy ⌐

The image of God brings an interesting possibility to mind. Could it be that Lucifer (who became Satan) rebelled against God's throne to set up his own kingdom because he was jealous? The Bible says that until Adam, Lucifer was closest to God of all the hosts of heaven (Isaiah 14:12). From other Scripture, we know that Lucifer was the guardian of the worship of God. It's hard to imagine, but he was more brilliant and beautiful than all the hosts of heaven!

But he must have witnessed the creation of Adam, or at least knew of the plans of Adam's creation. He must have known Adam would produce countless living souls who would also have the image and life of God Himself.

Imagine the prime minister of a great kingdom who is closer to the king than all of the royal subjects. But the prime minister becomes resentful of the young prince, who is heir to the throne, because the prince will soon take the prime minister's place at the right side of the king's throne.

Lucifer lost all his glory and was cast out of heaven forever. He will never witness the glory of

God again. He will witness only his own final judgment. No wonder he despises mankind so much and wants to destroy our hope of inheriting the kingdom! One day, though, we will look at Satan with mocking amusement and say, "You've got to be kidding!" Even Isaiah 14:16 says, "Is this the man that made the earth to tremble, that did shake kingdoms."

Seriously, we shouldn't make light of Satan's ability to oppress us and destroy souls, because he is committed to it. But we shouldn't fear him either! We are safe as long as we stay close to the One who has all authority in heaven and earth, and as long as we use the weapons He gives us. Satan is a tragic figure of self-destruction that deserves no pity. After all, he only exists to spread evil and disobedience to God. There is nothing else for him to do! He has no hope, and no redemption is possible for him because there can be no redeemer for fallen angels.

⌐ THE TRUTH ABOUT FALLEN ANGELS ¬

It isn't wrong to wonder why fallen angels can't be saved, especially in light of the fact that a fallen man can be saved. It's not that God didn't love His angelic host, including the fallen angels before the time they fell. Let me share with you one of the reasons why fallen angels are lost forever; a reason that greatly highlights the significance of the blood.

No redemption is possible for fallen angels because they have no blood. I realize that sounds simplistic, but, more specifically, they have no bloodline. They didn't descend from an original angel from whom they all shared a common lineage. They are not kin to each other. God created them the way a woodworker builds cabinets— each one similar to the others but separate and unique in some way. The angels are all similar creatures, and they do have a common purpose and value—a common glory in God—but they have no heritage, as we define the word heritage. They share a great fellowship of glorious service to God, but they aren't a family in the same way that mankind is a family. And as the book of Ruth and other parts of the Bible show, a redeemer must be a kinsman—a member of the family whose heritage needs redeeming

(Numbers 5:8; Ruth 2:19, 3:5).

For the angels to be redeemed they would have to be kin, and another kinsman angel would have to be their redeemer. But even if the angels were family, the redeeming angel would have to qualify in two additional ways. Before we look at these qualifications, let's do a little background research.

⌐ THE KINSMAN REDEEMER ¬

In Israel, the Law made it possible for a family to recover a heritage (usually land) that had been lost for whatever reason. In the story of Ruth, it appears there was some property that had been lost to the family of Naomi's husband, Elimelech. Perhaps Elimelech had borrowed money, using the property as collateral, so he could move his family to the country of Moab during the famine in Israel. Elimelech and both his sons died in Moab, leaving Naomi alone with her two daughters-in-law and no way to reclaim the family property. If, in fact, no property was involved, then at the very least Elimelech's family line would end since there were no sons. In any case, a family heritage needed to be redeemed. The story of what happened is God's lesson to us about what He requires of a redeemer.

A kinsman redeemer, besides being a family member, must be able to pay the price necessary to redeem the heritage and have no debt of his own. If the would-be redeemer was himself a debtor, he couldn't qualify in the eyes of God and His Law to pay anyone else's debt. Finally, the kinsman redeemer must be freely willing to pay the debt. He couldn't be tricked into paying the debt and the payment couldn't be bribed or extorted out of him. In other words, a kinsman redeemer had to understand the price of redemption, he had to possess the price of it free and clear, and he had to offer it willingly and with no strings attached.

As I pointed out, the fallen angels have no common kinship that would allow a single kinsman redeemer to pay for and reclaim all that they lost in their collective rebellion.

You may be asking, "This is very interesting, but how does all this relate to Jesus being our redeemer? And how is this significant to the blood?" First, the key word in that question is that Jesus is our Redeemer. He paid once for all of us because our blood kinship with each other and with Jesus is part of our heritage from Adam. Jesus qualified as our Kinsman because He was a flesh and blood human like us; Jesus' flesh and blood originated from the same source as ours. He was born within the bloodline of Adam, and that's what makes Him our kin!

Isn't it amazing? Our kinship with Jesus isn't just symbolic by His being a man. We have literal blood kinship with Him! God can trace an unbroken line, either forwards or backwards (and often both); from any human who ever lived and wind up at Mary, the mother of Jesus. For most of us, it would be a very long, crooked, and meandering line. But it doesn't matter if my bloodline traces all the way down to Japheth, the son of Noah, before it turns back upward from Noah through his son, Shem, and continues to Mary. However winding, it is still an unbroken line that gives me kinship with the blood of Jesus.

For the sake of argument, we're not talking about direct ancestry. But I don't have to have direct ancestry from Mary to be a fellow member with Jesus in Adam's family. Mary is a distant family relation with whom I have a common heritage—a heritage that was lost by our original father, Adam. So Jesus, Mary's Son, qualifies in that way to be my Kinsman Redeemer in that great heritage. Praise God, it's in the blood.

Let's put to rest a lie Satan has thrown at the church from time to time. Mary wasn't just a surrogate mother; she didn't just give birth to some human-looking life form that just appeared in her womb one day. Mary provided her ovum for the body of Jesus; He was her flesh and blood. He was born the true son of Mary and without a human father. As Luke 1:35 says, the Spirit of God "overshadowed" Mary and somehow, by overriding nature, gave her a child. That unborn child with no human father was Immanuel— God dwelling with us.

But what about the rest of the qualifying factors—the willingness and ability to be a redeemer? Jesus, our Brother in the blood of Adam, chose willingly to pay our debt with His own life (John 10:17-18). Jesus was also able to pay the price to redeem our souls from death and hell because, to the end of His amazing life, He had no sin debt of His own. He was the spotless Lamb.

Our sin and the sin of Adam are the cause of our debt, and death is the payment for it (Genesis 2:17; Romans 5:12, 6:23).

⌐ BLOOD IS EVERYTHING ⌐

The significance of the blood of Adam and the blood of Jesus show the genius of God's plan for the redemption of Man and the restoration of our heritage of intimacy with God. The blood is the key to seeing it.

Sometimes you may hear someone say how unfair it is that all mankind was made guilty because of Adam's sin. They'll loudly proclaim, "It's not my fault Adam sinned! And even if I do commit sins in my own life, it's only because Adam passed on his fallen nature to me through my father! I can't help being a sinner!" It's all true. We're all sinners because our fathers were sinners, just like their fathers before them were sinners. It goes all the way back to Adam.

But here's the good news: Our shared guilt through the sin-stained blood of our fathers means we can have a shared righteousness through the righteous blood of a kinsman redeemer (Romans 5:19). The fact that we are able to inherit Adam's spiritual death makes possible a once-for-all sacrifice for the sin guilt of Adam's whole family. Read that again and underline it because it's the main significance of the blood of Adam. It was able to carry his heritage of God's image forward to every one of us. And even though Adam fell, we still have something of God's image in all of us. However, the life of God and our ability to know Him intimately were lost when Adam chose to remain intimate with his fallen wife instead of God.

A curse can only go forward in a bloodline; but a heritage that is redeemed by a true kinsman redeemer is returned to the entire family that lost it. We are the family of Adam, who lost our heritage of life and communion with God. Jesus, our Kinsman, bought it back for us.

But what if Adam and Eve had never disobeyed God? What if they had remained innocent and alive to God? Would we be "okay" now, never having need of a savior? Not likely; and the answer to that question reveals yet another layer of genius in God's restoration plan.

Sooner or later, someone would have brought the curse of death to everyone in the bloodline after them. And there might eventually have been many innocent bloodlines running parallel to many fallen bloodlines. In this situation, it is unlikely that one kinsman would be able to redeem the lost heritage of all the different bloodlines. But Adam and Eve didn't remain innocent. What matters is that innocence can be lost. God's unmerited grace cannot be lost.

⌐ GOD HAD A PLAN ¬

The Bible shows us that before the world began God intended to reveal Himself to man in a way that would free Him to relate to us on the basis of His grace, not on our innocence or ability to be faithful to Him. Revelation 13:8 says:

And all that dwell upon the earth shall worship him, whose names are not written in the book

of life of the Lamb slain from the foundation of
the world.

In hope of eternal life, which God, that cannot
lie, promised before the world began.
~ *TITUS 1:2*

Lucifer and a third of the angels were lost to
God forever because they lost their innocence.
Could that happen again among the remaining
angels? It's hard to imagine the possibility. The
apostle Paul said "Don't you know that we shall
judge angels?" (I Corinthians 6:3). That may
mean we will testify in the judgment against
those fallen spirits that oppressed us continually
in life! But it may also mean that because we cannot lose our relationship with Him, we will be
responsible for nurturing the eternal faithfulness
of our innocent, angelic, fellow servants.

But from the start of creation, God went to
work on a plan—He would destroy the power of
death, He would make it impossible to lose favor
with Him, and He would do it in a way that
would show the purity of His justice and the

unmatched greatness of His love. Our redemption was not a mopping up of something unexpectedly spilled. God's plan for our salvation was not His Plan B. There was never another plan.

The Bible makes clear that God is not the author of sin. But God is so infinite that He was able to use the evil jealousy and rage of Satan and his legions to shape history—down to the smallest detail—to accomplish His purposes.

In Part Two of this book, I'll teach you how God used Satan to help openly reveal Jesus as the promised Redeemer—the Redeemer who would set us free and restore our heritage of intimate relationship with God forever.

~ *Part Two* ~

THE RESTORATION

In the second part of the book, I want to teach you about the personal miracle of salvation. Much of this portion of the book will relate well with what you learned about the blood in Part One; but I want to focus more on Jesus Himself, His blood, His sacrifice, and what these things really mean for you.

⌐ THE LESSON OF NICODEMUS ¬

One of the best known stories about our Savior is in the book of John, which tells how Nicodemus stole into the night to seek out Jesus. He was confused yet moved by Jesus and His powerful works. He must have been troubled by the effect Jesus had on him because we see him going to Jesus in secret under the cover of night. Nicodemus, a leader of Israel in Jerusalem, was afraid to speak with Jesus in public during the day. Can you visualize Nicodemus, glancing over his shoulder as he approached Jesus to speak to Him? Here's the scene from John, chapter 3:

> *There was a man of the Pharisees, named Nicodemus, a ruler of the Jews: The same came to Jesus by night, and said unto him, Rabbi, we know that thou art a teacher come from God: for no man can do these miracles that thou doest, except God be with him. Jesus answered and said unto him, Verily, verily, I say unto thee, Except a man be born again, he cannot see the kingdom of God. Nicodemus saith unto him, How can a man be born when he is old? can he enter the second time into his mother's womb, and be born? Jesus answered, Verily, verily, I say unto thee, Except a man be born of water and of the Spirit, he cannot enter into the kingdom of God. That which is born of the flesh is*

flesh; and that which is born of the Spirit is spirit. Marvel not that I said unto thee, Ye must be born again. The wind bloweth where it listeth, and thou hearest the sound thereof, but canst not tell whence it cometh, and whither it goeth: so is every one that is born of the Spirit. Nicodemus answered and said unto him, How can these things be? Jesus answered and said unto him, Art thou a master of Israel, and knowest not these things?

~ JOHN 3:1-10

The affect upon Nicodemus of seeing Jesus perform miracles reminds me of the direct way God first revealed Himself to the Children of Israel when they were slaves in Egypt. The time had come that God chose to deliver Israel from bondage. First, He revealed His name through Moses. Then, He revealed His power by signs through Moses—plagues upon Egypt and miracles in the wilderness. The planned affect was to silence unbelief. That's why God uses miracles. Miracles are not for the believer. They are for the unbeliever.

So Nicodemus, a responsible leader whom all of Israel respected, decided to take his troubled soul to Jesus. But he wasn't honest with Jesus; He decided to cushion himself by flattering Jesus with recognition as God's messenger and even assured Him that his peers knew it too. Jesus ignored his flattery and, without mentioning the miracles, aimed straight at Nicodemus's self-assurance, saying, "Verily, verily I say unto thee, except a man be born again he cannot see the kingdom of God." Can you imagine the odd look of confusion on Nicodemus's face when he heard those words?

If the true reason Nicodemus was there with Jesus was to recognize Him as sent from God, he would have paused and realized that Jesus was sharing something extraordinary with him and that he should listen. Instead, Nicodemus was defensive, and he fired back with evidence of his lack of understanding: "Well, how can a man be born when he is old? Can he come through his mother's womb a second time and be born?"

Nevertheless, Jesus was patient with Nicodemus and opened the door of heaven for him:

"Verily, verily I say unto thee, except a man be born of water and of the Spirit he cannot enter into the kingdom of God." Jesus must have loved Nicodemus, for in the Gospels we don't see much tenderness between Jesus and the religious leaders in Jerusalem. The passage in John, chapter 3 seems like a short sketch of a much longer conversation they must have had. During that conversation, Jesus spoke what are probably the most quoted words in the Bible: "For God so loved the world, that he gave his only begotten Son, that whosoever believeth in him should not perish, but have everlasting life" (John 3:16).

The entire gospel message was laid out for Nicodemus that evening in order to show him that Jesus was more than a teacher from God. Jesus spoke directly into Nicodemus's soul, and Nicodemus must have been changed forever.

After that secret meeting in the night, Nicodemus was probably seeing the kingdom of heaven all around him. The Spirit-anointed gospel of Jesus Christ has that kind of power over the hearts of tough-minded skeptics. But the gospel must be aimed at their hearts, even though skeptics tend to live in their minds.

During that brief meeting, Jesus took aim at Nicodemus's dishonest self-assurance and still opened his eyes to truth. Jesus didn't rebuke Nicodemus for his sarcasm about being born a second time. He simply showed him the meaning of new birth: A man must be born of water and the Spirit.

Later, in John 19:39, we see the bold and loving evidence of Nicodemus's lesson. This passage makes a point of mentioning that Nicodemus "first came to Jesus by night." But after Jesus' body was removed from the cross, Nicodemus was there to care for it with myrrh and aloes, openly showing his respect and devotion. Why would he take this risk if he didn't believe Jesus was who he said he was?

Some have taught that "born of water" means water baptism that occurs after you've been saved. But that's not the context of the passage. Nicodemus had mistaken the second birth Jesus mentioned as a second natural birth into the world. Then Jesus shared the difference between the "spiritual" birth and the "natural" one.

⌐ BORN OF WATER AND SPIRIT ⌐

You must be born of water and then of the spirit. You are first born of water as you enter this world in the flesh. Jesus even clarified this by saying, "That which is of the flesh is flesh. That which is of the spirit is spirit." We must be born of the spirit. But no one is born of the spirit unless they are first born of water. Are you a little confused? I'll explain. Remember that angels, although empowered to take on material form, are not flesh. They were not born of water. Other creatures on the earth (aside from man) are born of water, but they cannot be born of the Spirit. In fact, all of creation started with water in some form as God moved over the face of the waters and glorified it into distinct bodies of creation (Genesis 1:2).

You were immersed in water in your mother's womb as God's creative power moved within it to form you; your body and its blood are up to 70% water; you are literally born of water. Your birth into the world was, in a sense, your first water baptism, because it proclaimed you as rightfully born into the family of man.

But you also need a second birth; a spiritual birth into Christ in order to be alive to God. This is necessary because, as a descendent of Adam, you were born spiritually dead.

Remember: You were first born of water—that which is flesh is flesh. But without a second birth, the curse you inherited demands your blood to pay for your sin—the sin you inherited and the sins you've committed. You must be born of water and of the spirit to be fully alive, to know God, and to see His kingdom.

Jesus Christ was born of water through Mary so He could be one of us—our Kinsman. He didn't just come to earth and appear in the form of a man. He entered the world in a legitimate way—born of a woman. If He had not entered the world through the proper doorway of birth, He would not have been able to become a doorway of life for us (John 10:1-9). He could not have qualified as the Kinsman Redeemer for us.

After Jesus died, a Roman soldier pierced His side, and from that wound poured a mixture of water and blood. The water proclaimed that Jesus was a true man, born in the flesh, a horrifying fact to Satan and the fallen angels.

In his first epistle, John shows us that any spirit which is from God will openly declare that Jesus Christ has come in the flesh. All spirits that are not of God either will not or cannot declare this (I John 4:3). The fallen angels despise this truth—they fear and despise the humanity of Jesus. Throughout the history of the church, Satan has stirred up false teachers, false prophets, factions, and movements that have tried to cast doubt on the humanity of Jesus.

As I mentioned earlier, Satan himself identified Jesus as the Son of God and as the flesh and blood Christ. He spends most of his time now trying to get us to deny it.

But Jesus has come in the flesh, He died a man's death, and He rose again on the third day because He was also God and had the power to take up His life again. After taking upon Himself all the bloodguilt of the world, He conquered death and rose again, holy and blameless, to glorious new life. By faith in His work, we receive the same power to be raised to life from spiritual death. We have the power to rise from the grave when He returns.

⌐ THE IMPORTANCE OF WITNESS ¬

The entire spiritual realm, holy and fallen, was there to recognize that Jesus Christ has come in the flesh, and He did qualify to be our Redeemer. The holy angels of God proclaimed it in the sheep-grazing fields to the lowest of the working class in Israel. You see, shepherds were seen as unfaithful to the Law of Moses because they couldn't observe the feasts and sacrifices as faithfully as everyone else. Their sheep, after all, required their constant attention and protection. They were outcast from the "upright" (make that "uptight") community. These outcasts were chosen to witness the greatest proclamation of good news in the history of the world. No doubt, the sky was filled with brilliant light, but only these lowly shepherds saw and heard the rejoicing of the heavenly host.

God the Son, Maker of all creation, was now present in the world. He was present in a way that had never before existed—both gloriously and humbly. He was present to be one of us, to live like us, to grow and learn like us. He would suffer disappointment and temptation, just as we have and do. But He would preserve His innocence by overcoming temptation through trusting submission to the Father. Hebrews 4:15 says, "For we have not an high priest which cannot be touched with the feeling of our infirmities; but was in all points tempted like as we are, yet without sin."

By the age of twelve, Jesus knew His purpose and who He really was, but He also faithfully submitted to His parents.

> *And he said unto them, How is it that ye sought me? wist ye not that I must be about my Father's business? And they understood not the saying which he spake unto them. And he went down with them, and came to Nazareth, and was subject unto them: but his mother kept all these sayings in her heart. And Jesus increased in wisdom and stature, and in favour with God and man.*
>
> ~ *LUKE 2:49-52*; emphasis mine

Jesus grew into manhood at the carpenter's bench of Joseph, to whom He submitted as a son. Through Joseph, His surrogate father, Jesus was the legal descendent of David and heir to his throne. Through Mary, His biological mother, Jesus was the blood descendent of David. But more than this, the Spirit of God Himself pronounced Jesus the Son of God on the day He went into the desert to be baptized by His cousin, John.

> *And Jesus, when he was baptized, went up straightway out of the water: and, lo, the heavens were opened unto him, and he saw the Spirit of God descending like a dove, and lighting upon him: And lo a voice from heaven, saying, This is my beloved Son, in whom I am well pleased.*
>
> ~ MATTHEW 3:16-4:1

The scene described in the above verse was an incredible moment. It wasn't just a gushing, sentimental word from God, voicing His adoring affection and pride in His Son. It was a time-stopping, universe-silencing announcement. God was presenting Jesus to the heavens and the earth and verifying Him as the Son of God with all of creation as witnesses.

When someone makes a claim about their birthright, authority, or any other claim of status others may challenge, a known authority must verify that claim. As I described above, the host of heaven witnessed to the natural birth of Jesus as the Son of God. It was on record in the spiritual realm to be used in the judgment when all the wicked of men and angels are condemned. Then, at the baptism, the Father witnessed to the Sonship of Jesus and anointed Jesus to fulfill His will—that is also on record before all of creation.

⌐ SATAN'S PLAN ¬

Even Satan witnessed to who Jesus was and the legitimacy of His claim to become the Kinsman Redeemer for mankind. However, it was not Satan's intention to be a witness. He wanted to be a spoiler.

Satan was aware of the special circumstances under which Jesus was born. He saw the anointing of Jesus at His baptism and heard the witness of the Father proclaiming His Son. Since Satan is an angel, he is more intelligent than we can understand. But he is also somewhat blinded by his rage and evil intentions. It was only after witnessing what happened at the baptism of Jesus that Satan could be sure that the promised Redeemer was to be God the Son Himself. Satan finally understood that all the fuss over the baptism of Jesus meant the baptism was really the coronation of a king, and it was being witnessed to by heaven. But Satan still didn't get the big picture.

> But we speak the wisdom of God in a mystery, even the hidden wisdom, which God ordained before the world unto our glory: Which none of the princes of this world knew: for had they known it, they would not have crucified the Lord of glory.
>
> ~ 1 CORINTHIANS 2:7-8

Satan knew the Scriptures. He knew about the promised Redeemer since the first mention of Him recorded in Genesis 3:15. He knew what the

Messiah-Redeemer was supposed to accomplish.

> *Seventy weeks are determined upon thy people and upon thy holy city, to finish the transgression, and to make an end of sins, and to make reconciliation for iniquity, and to bring in everlasting righteousness, and to seal up the vision and prophecy, and to anoint the most Holy.*
>
> ~ *DANIEL 9:24*

Satan knew the Redeemer would somehow restore peace on the earth through a kingdom and deliver Man from the bondage and guilt of sin. Basically, the Redeemer would undo everything he had done and also destroy him. But he was blind to how it would be accomplished. Nevertheless, when Jesus was baptized, Satan realized that the time had come and that the Redeemer-King had been officially revealed.

There were only two ways Satan could stop what was coming and keep his dominion. He could try to disqualify Jesus from being our Kinsman Redeemer ... or kill Him.

It wouldn't have been Satan's first choice to

kill Jesus, since he would then be guilty of spilling innocent blood—and the blood of the Son of God, no less. Up to that point, all the torment Satan had inflicted upon the world had been within his legal right to inflict. The world dominion, after all, was his; the world he dominated wasn't innocent. Even Paul claimed we were enemies of God when he said, "For if, when we were enemies, we were reconciled to God by the death of his Son, much more, being reconciled, we shall be saved by his life" (Romans 5:10).

Satan didn't want to add the murder of innocent blood to his list of crimes against God. Ultimately, though, that is exactly what he did when he failed to disqualify Jesus as the Kinsman Redeemer. Luke 4:1-13 is a lengthy passage about how Satan tried to disqualify Jesus, so I won't include it here. But I strongly urge you to pick up your Bible and read it before you continue, because the next section shows how God used Satan to witness to who Jesus was.

Many people have struggled with questions about the temptation of Jesus and have come to different conclusions about what Satan was trying to accomplish. We know Satan is crafty and persuasive; his most frightening weapon against us is our own willingness to be deceived and misguided. He uses our fears, resentments, character flaws, appetites, and anything else he can learn about us in order to lead us into acting independent of God. And he uses something attractive to lure us into a trap. In the wilderness, he targeted the longings of Jesus. Satan wanted to lure Jesus into doing things that would disqualify Him as our Kinsman Redeemer.

SATAN FALLS INTO HIS OWN TRAP

The first attempt to disqualify Jesus simply involved tempting Him to break His fast. It had been forty days of fasting, which is a scripturally-appropriate time to break a long fast. But Satan suggested that Jesus command the earth to give Him bread out of the stones. This shows that Satan knew who Jesus was, and he also knew Jesus would be able to do it at will. Jesus was God in the flesh; it would not have been wrong. After all, Jesus would soon turn water into wine, so what's the difference?

Satan wasn't suggesting that Jesus pray to God and then receive bread from the stones by faith. Satan wanted Jesus to act independently of God and command the stones out of His pre-incarnate authority—He had the authority to do it. But it would have meant Jesus wasn't living as a man anymore. To be our Redeemer, He must be our Kinsman in this earthly life—nothing more or less. Jesus not only had to be born as we are, He had to live as we are called to live so He could fully identify with us in the eyes of God's pure justice.

We are called to live daily by faith in the trustworthiness of God. Everything Jesus did in His life, even the miracles, the Father did through Him as He exercised faith. Does that surprise you?

> *Then answered Jesus and said unto them, Verily, verily, I say unto you,* The Son can do nothing *of himself, but what he seeth the Father do: for what things soever he doeth, these also doeth the Son likewise.*
>
> ~ *JOHN 5:19* ; emphasis mine

Let this mind be in you, which was also in Christ Jesus: Who, being in the form of God, thought it not robbery to be equal with God: But made himself of no reputation, and took upon him the form of a servant, and was made in the likeness of men: And being found in fashion as a man, he humbled himself, and became obedient unto death, even the death of the cross.

~ *PHILIPPIANS 2 : 5 - 8*

Everything Jesus did in life was an act of obedience. He lived only out of His humanity. Satan wanted Jesus to do something—anything—out of His divinity. But Jesus didn't confront the intentions of the tempter. Instead, He answered with the Word of God and waited upon the Father.

Next, Satan carried Jesus to the top of a high mountain and showed Him the kingdoms of the world. He knew the purpose of Jesus was to build a kingdom and restore the earth to a garden. "Well here's a short cut, Jesus. You can have it all right now," Satan offered. "I never really wanted this world anyway. All I truly want is a little recognition. I'll get out of the way right now without a fight. Nobody has to suffer anymore. Just give me a little recognition. Show me I'm worth something. Worship me just once."

We don't know if Satan used these words, but the nature of the temptation shows he knew some of the heartache Jesus had. Jesus was so intimate with the Father, He had the same longing to gather His people in unity and peace under His wings (Matthew 23:37-38; Luke 19:41-44).

The manner in which Jesus answered, however, shows what would have happened if Satan had succeeded. "Get thee behind me, Satan: for it is written, Thou shalt worship the Lord thy God, and him only shalt thou serve" (Luke 4:5; Deuteronomy 6:13).

It angered Jesus for Satan to use His love in order to tempt Him to sin against God. Kneeling to worship Satan would have put Jesus in debt to the Law of God. Jesus would no longer qualify to pay for the redemption of Man because He Himself would be a debtor in need of redemption.

Having failed in his attack on the obvious things, Satan became clever. He attempted to confuse Jesus in His will; he took Jesus to the top of the temple. From high on the pinnacle, they could look down upon the entire city where, directly below, were hundreds of people. All the business of the temple buzzed below, while the very One to whom all that business pointed was standing above them, longing to be known, longing to hear them cry out "Blessed is He who comes in the name of the Lord." Just days prior to His crucifixion, Jesus left the temple for the last time, speaking out His desire to hear those very words (Matthew 23:39).

Atop that high place, Satan suggested that if Jesus were to leap from the temple, the angels would prevent Him from dashing His foot on the stones below; they would bare Him up. Satan quoted from a passage of Scripture all of Israel knew pointed to the Messiah (Psalm 91:12). Satan must have known that bypassing any part of the Redeemer's work would put an end to it. If Jesus had leaped from the temple and floated gently to the courtyard, it would have been an unmistakable sign of who He was. Israel would have had to accept their Messiah as a king, and that would have been good enough for Satan. There would have been no Redeemer—just a king. Most of the people during that time would have rejoiced in seeing Jesus appear as Messiah the king; but again, no one would have been redeemed (Matthew 26:53-54). Jesus was born to become Prophet, Priest, and King. Without the cross, He could not be a Priest; He could not go before the throne of God, offering His blood on our behalf.

The fate of man hung in the balance. Would He follow His longing to bring peace to Jerusalem, unite Israel, bless the people (including His mother), and avoid the suffering of the cross? Or would He accept the stripes, the nails, and the hell of absorbing all the sin and guilt of the world? Well, we know what He chose, and it was freely His choice. Nothing was forced upon Him.

When Peter attacked the temple guard the night Jesus was arrested in the Garden of Gethsemane, Jesus rebuked Peter for not understanding that He could call on His Father to defend Him, if He so desired. Twelve legions of angels would have, to put it lightly, instantly settled the matter (Matthew 26:53). But Jesus answered Satan as a man should—a man who knows that we are not supposed to use the promises of God as leverage in order to move Him; but rather trust those promises as our source of blessing and deliverance.

The Redeemer who would fulfill the Daniel 9:24 prophecy (see page 41), must be a natural Kinsman of man. He must live as nothing more than a man so that His identification with man could not be challenged. He must be unspotted with sin. He must willingly choose to pay the price of redemption without any coercion. The price Jesus chose to pay was to take our sin and death into His innocent blood, and then spill it upon the earth.

Satan unwittingly testified in the open that Jesus was the Promised One of God. When the fallen angels face their final judgment before the throne of God they'll have no way to challenge the qualifications or identity of our Redeemer.

⌐ HE PAID OUR DEBT ¬

These things have I written unto you that believe

on the name of the Son of God; that ye may
know that ye have eternal life, and that ye may
believe on the name of the Son of God.

~ 1 JOHN 5:13

There is so much that could be taught from the above verse. The main truth in it is about hope. Man usually thinks of hope as the possibility of something good. The kind of hope God gives is the assurance of things that are certain. He graciously established the hope of eternal life before the world began (Titus 1:2). He fulfilled it and made it certain in the finished work of Jesus. And by "believing on" this hope (which means to trust in it), we make it ours. It's a sure thing; we can know we have eternal life.

John's point is also that we have eternal life from the moment we're saved. In Christ we don't wait for eternal life—we have it. That's because, as Paul also taught, our old life dies with Jesus when we are reborn with His life (Galatians 2:20). According to Luke 19:10, Jesus came "to seek and to save that which was lost."

In the above verse Luke gives us the simplest

explanation of the gospel. It begins with the fact that we are lost. We've already looked closely at how this happened and what it means for us. Sin brought death to the spirit of Adam so there was no spiritual life for him to pass on to us. Sin also brought death to Adam, which he did pass on to us by way of his blood. A dead spirit and dying blood are the prices of sin; but Jesus became sin and death on the cross so His blood could pay for our sin. He did it so we wouldn't have to pay for it with our own blood. Jesus challenges us to trust in the value of His blood and trust in no other payment for our sin. If we respond to His call, we are made clean of our sin and can receive His life in our spirits.

Ephesians 2:8 says "by grace you have been saved through faith." The Greek word for "saved" means rescued. Through faith in the blood of Jesus, we can be rescued from a destiny we can't escape on our own. Our dead spirits can be resurrected. When we are born again, the Holy Spirit of God breathes new life into us so right now we can truly know Him the way He desires. And this new life is just a sample of the glory God has for us in heaven when our lives on earth have ended.

But those who die without this new life must go to the only other place God has prepared. It wasn't prepared for them specifically, but there's no other place to go. It's a place so gruesomely separated from the glory of God that the Hebrews named it after the place outside of Jerusalem where garbage is burned. The English Bible calls it "hell." But again, hell was not meant for man.

⌐ THE REALITY OF HELL ⌐

Then shall he say also unto them on the left hand, Depart from me, ye cursed, into everlasting fire, prepared for the devil and his angels.

~ MATTHEW 25:41

Hell was created for Satan and the fallen angels. They are eternally separated from the glory they had with God before their rebellion, and they are living out their eternal death now while they make every effort to lure us into rebellion against God. The only rescue we have is to be born again.

Imagine that you are lost. Jesus finds you and keeps you with Him so you don't get lost again. Actually, everyone is hopelessly lost and Jesus is the only way out. Unfortunately, most people don't understand how badly lost they are. They would probably admit that they feel a little lost at times, but they want to find their own way out. On their own, they'll never find the life and victory Jesus offers, but they keep on searching. They hack their way through a jungle of ideas, religions, distractions, ambitions, sin, and even good causes. If one path through the jungle doesn't lead them to what they're seeking, they'll start hacking out another path. All the while, Jesus keeps calling out, "Hey, I'm here! Just stay where you are. Be still and call out to Me. I'll find you. I'll take you out of here to where you'll have more to rejoice about than you can imagine."

That's really the way it is! The only way we can stop living a lost life is to be found by Jesus. And the only way we can be found by Him is to respond to His call. We have to come out of hiding and call out to Jesus, whom God has sent to find us.

If you're praying for those who are lost, pray that they will give up trying to save themselves. Pray that they will accept their lost state and admit they can't find their way on their own. Only then will they be able to respond to Jesus calling in the distance. There is no battle we must fight to reach Jesus; He is as close as our breath.

But sometimes there is a battle in the heart. It's hard to break through barriers like pride, fear, resentment, and selfish ambition in order to respond to Jesus. Sometimes this battle is necessary, and God will use it to soften a willful heart. When stubborn people are pursued by God this way, eventually they come to a place where they realize their way isn't working; they feel like giving up; they feel down and broken hearted. They hear themselves saying words like, "Things will never change, no matter how hard I try." Believe it or not, this is a good place for a lost person to be! It isn't that being lost or failing to find what they're looking for is good, but they may not be finding it because God doesn't want them to work out their lives without Him. Jesus said "I am the way, the truth, and the life: no one cometh unto the Father, but by me" (John 14:6).

When we are finally ready to surrender our hearts to Jesus, we must meet Him with nothing to offer Him in trade for saving us. We must accept it as a free gift paid for by His broken body and blood. If we try to add anything to it, we insult the value of His sacrifice.

We must not try to hide anything from Jesus about how lost we are. Believe me, He knows far better than we do how great our struggles and failures are. Missionary and author Jack Miller used to put it this way, "Relax, you're worse than you think. But you're loved far more than you'll ever understand."

One more thing: Jesus is our only hope. There are no alternatives, so it's a waste of time thinking about other options. Jesus has taken care of everything; He has given all of Himself to us. He is simply calling us to give ourselves to Him.

It is simple enough for a child to understand and accept. But it's the simplicity that also makes it so hard for our self-centered minds to accept. It's just too easy. We humans, especially hard working adults, tend to think we must deserve what we get. So we try to earn God's grace before we accept it. And we deny it to some whom we think are forever unworthy. The unvarnished truth is that we are all unworthy. No one could earn a single hair from the head of Jesus. And without His blood we would all get what we deserve.

⌐ THE VALUE OF HIS BLOOD ⌐

Imagine that you alone own an irreplaceable and precious object that could save a dying tribe of people whom you have never seen. After a time of painful soul-searching, you decide you must give up that precious thing. You'll never again feel the joy of owning it; you'll never be able to leave it to your children. As you watch that precious thing leave your grasp, wouldn't you want it to have as much value as possible? The more you could see being accomplished by your precious sacrifice, the less anguish you would feel and the more comfort you would have. And how precious do you think your sacrifice would be in the eyes of those it rescued?

There is a true story of a bus driver who lost his brakes as he was carrying people down a steep gorge road in a third-world country. The driver was unable to downshift as the bus picked up speed. All he could do was try to keep the bus on the road until they crossed over the narrow, one-lane bridge at the bottom, after which the bus would eventually slow to a stop. But as the out-of-control bus neared the bridge, the driver could see a small figure standing in the middle of it, looking over the rail at the river below. His heart sank and he knew he had to choose: run the bus off the road into the gorge below and probably kill everyone on board or run over what became clear to the driver was a young boy who had no way of escape. There was little time to think; but the driver knew what had to happen. So he gazed at the boy without blinking until he disappeared under the bus. As the bus gradually slowed to a stop, the people on board railed at the driver for not being able to stop the bus. "How could you run over that poor creature and do nothing?" they demanded.

But the driver could barely hear them through

his own sobbing. "That was not a poor creature," he cried. "That was my son." And then the cost of their salvation became clear. He gave up the life of the one he loved most to save the lives of many.

Jesus hates our sin and death so much He gave up more than we can ever comprehend in order to rescue us from them. On the cross, He gave up His own innocent life as a man and His unbroken communion with the Father and Spirit. So I ask you: How much value do you think God wants the blood of Jesus to have? How angry do you think it makes Him when we hesitate to accept what He paid so much to buy for us?

⌐ A NEW SONG ⌐

John tells us in Revelation that the blood of Jesus will be the main inspiration for worship in eternity.

And they sung a new song, saying, Thou art worthy to take the book, and to open the seals thereof: for thou wast slain, and hast redeemed

us to God by thy blood out of every kindred, and
tongue, and people, and nation.

~ *REVELATION 5:9*

The majesty of the blood of Jesus is so great that for all eternity in heaven we will grow in our understanding and celebration of it. We will worship Jesus and the power of His blood as we see more clearly how deep and wide and high the love of Jesus is (Ephesians 3:17-19).

If there is anyone whose sins are too great for the cross to redeem, then it would mean the blood of Jesus has limited value—an unthinkable notion. Who would dare say such a thing to God's face? But people do say things like, "God couldn't possibly forgive me now" or "I can't just accept forgiveness for the things I've done and act like they never happened."

His sacrifice has limitless value, and all the sins of the world—from chattering gossip to the blackest abominations throughout all of history—were laid on Jesus. He died with them on His soul, and His resurrection from the dead is our assurance that all those sins have been forgiven.

There is only one thing left that will send a person to hell: the unforgivable sin of rejecting God's Son and His sacrifice to the end of his or her life.

~ Part Three ~

THE KINGDOM
HAS COME

But if I cast out devils by the Spirit of God,
then the kingdom of God is come unto you.

~ *MATTHEW* 12:28

With this new life in Jesus, we can know God as He desires to be known. We are alive to Him again. And we must be spiritually alive to God in order to see His kingdom. Now remember, when Jesus spoke to Nicodemus about seeing the Kingdom, He wasn't just talking about a place. It's not just Heaven—it's the Kingdom of Heaven. Heaven is where God will fellowship forever with the redeemed and all the Holy angels. The Kingdom of Heaven is God's rulership, and believers can begin living in the Kingdom of Heaven the moment they are saved.

We don't wait for eternal life with God. The Bible says believers already have eternal life that was prepared before the world began (Titus 1:2; I John 5:13). We practice living in the kingdom when we remember who we are in Jesus, when we remember where our home is, and when we allow that to change how we live, talk, work, serve, and face challenges.

The kingdom is God's way of doing things. We practice living in the kingdom when we do things God's way; when we say, "Yes, Lord," and refuse to doubt. And if we live our lives that way, we take the kingdom of God with us wherever we go. We are called to spread the kingdom and expand it, even while the world is dying and heading for judgment.

When Jesus preached about the kingdom, He said, "Repent; the kingdom of God has come" (Matthew 4:17). So God's way of doing things (His system) is in operation right now. The Greek word Jesus used for "see" in John 3:3 means to have revelation understanding—a deep level of knowing that is given by the Holy Spirit. Paul prayed for the Ephesian church that God would give them "the spirit of wisdom and revelation in the knowledge of Him" (Ephesians 1:17).

The word Paul used for "revelation" is the same word John used in his last book of the Bible, calling it the Revelation of Jesus Christ. The word apocalypse is also derived from that word, and it means to have the veil removed. But unless you are born again, the spirit can't remove the veil from over your eyes so you can see God's kingdom. And if you can't see God's kingdom, you can't have the wisdom needed to operate in it.

That's why it's mostly a waste of time trying to explain to someone who's not saved why believers do what we do. They don't understand why we bring in the tithe; they don't understand why we lay hands on the sick. They are not born again. They don't have revelation. Their eyes are covered. The Bible says "no man can declare Jesus Lord but by the Holy Spirit" (1 Corinthians 12:3). And Jesus said, "... no man can come unto me, except it were given unto him of my Father" (John 6:65).

The Word of God says that we are all naturally blind. We cannot see; but then God uses our lives to prepare us for revelation. This happens continually in a believer's life as well. The Holy Spirit, in His own time, will lift the veil from every area of blindness we walk in. When that happens, we can say "Yes!" to Jesus and receive increased wisdom to walk in the kingdom. So, let's look more deeply into what it means to live in the kingdom.

SAVED FOR AN ABUNDANT LIFE

I believe that God doesn't just want us saved from hell. He wants us saved from defeat and death during this life. John 10:10 says the thief cometh to kill, steal, and destroy. But Jesus has come to give you life and life more abundantly. He wants you safe from damnation here on Earth. He wants you safe from disease. He wants to rescue you from it. That's why He gave us a full covenant of peace, a covenant of promise, and a covenant of eternity in Heaven. If all God wanted was for you to go to heaven, then He would save you and end your life so you'd go immediately to heaven. But God wants you to live abundantly here in this life. Look up John 10:10 in your Bible. It says, "I am come that they might have life, and that they might have it more abundantly."

It makes perfect sense that Jesus wouldn't defeat death by dying for us until He had also overcome the world by victoriously living for us. When we're saved, we don't just benefit from the Lord's death. We receive all the power of His victorious life. In fact, He plainly said that we, as His Body, have enough of His power available to see even greater victories and do greater works than He performed (John 14:12).

Again, Ephesians 2:8 says by grace you've been saved. But, remember, when God saves that which is lost, He restores as well. You aren't just saved from death and hell; you are restored to life and freedom. And it's by the grace of God that this happens. You don't earn it. You must believe Jesus is who He says He is, and you must be willing to accept forgiveness and restoration as free gifts of God.

So the point is, we see the kingdom and walk in the kingdom the same way we are born into the kingdom. We walk by the grace of God through faith in the finished work of our Redeemer, Jesus Christ. And there's more than enough of God's grace to save and restore all who will call upon Jesus.

But even after saving and restoring us, the work of God's grace is not finished! God's grace is at work in us, through faith in the blood of Jesus, to transform us. Paul reminds us what unredeemed hearts and lives can become (Ephesians 2:1-3; Galatians 5:19-21). Look it up! Find out what Paul says!

We can easily become greedy, jealous, and even murderous. Even if we never murdered someone with a weapon, there are times when each of us has murdered a soul with the tongue. We've taken life out of some people with words. A person's heart can be killed with words. Paul reminds us of our roots. But thank God that He is our mighty, amazing, and unchanging God, and that His grace has the power to transform us into generous people who speak life into others!

So God's grace doesn't just save us from the hell we deserve for our greed, jealousy, and murder. He saves us from being greedy, jealous, and murderous. We can rejoice in the blessings and promises from God through the blood of Jesus if we'll just proclaim them without doubting or letting our circumstances have the last word. The most precious is His promise to transform us into the very character of Jesus (Romans 8:29).

⌐ PLEADING THE BLOOD ¬

My dear friend and renowned gospel artiste, Vicki Winans, tells a story that illustrates the power of "pleading the blood." To those who have never heard this phrase, it may sound a little strange. We usually think the word "plead" means to ask or beg. Sometimes we think we are "pleading" when we pray to God for deliverance from something. But you'll better understand the real meaning of "pleading the blood" after I share Vicki's story.

Her son, "Coconut," had been going through a difficult phase in which his walk with the Lord was not as strong as his mother would have liked. Late one night while walking on the streets of New York, he was held at gunpoint by a crazed criminal. Coconut lay face down on the cold sidewalk, helpless and terrified, his assailant's foot pressing firmly into his back and a gun to his head. He went cold as the angry gunman growled that he was about to die.

He thought about begging for his life, but Coconut remembered what he learned in church and from his mother. He cried out "The blood of Jesus!" Louder, he shouted, "The blood of Jesus! The blood of Jesus!" The agitated attacker cursed him and tried to fire the gun, but it wouldn't fire! Freaked out by the desperate, repetitious wailing of the young man, the gunman fled in terror.

This heroic example of the power of pleading the blood reminds me of John's vision recorded in the book of Revelation: "They overcame Him by the blood of the Lamb and the word of their testimony" (12:11).

What makes the blood of Jesus so powerful? What is it that enables even the simple phrase 'the blood of Jesus' to produce such supernatural results?

For the most part, the blood of Jesus is a mystery to us. Even in eternity, we will be discovering its power and significance. But with the guidance of the Holy Spirit, we can receive everything God has prepared for us to have in this life. We can plead the blood of Jesus, and we don't have to have full understanding of it to be covered by it.

As I have already described, blood is central to God's plan for the redemption of mankind and the destruction of sin and death. The blood is our exodus from bondage and our deliverance from the wilderness of sin to the promised land of freedom and glory.

In Exodus, when God demonstrated His wrath against the Egyptians, blood was used as a statement of faith in God's provision of deliverance for those in covenant with Him.

> . . . when He seeth the blood upon the lintel, and
> on the two side posts, the Lord will pass over the
> door, and will not suffer the destroyer to come in

unto your houses to smite you.

~*EXODUS 12:23*

The children of Israel couldn't have understood the spiritual significance of putting the blood on their doors, and they couldn't have known anything about the future Redeemer, which the blood represented. But they didn't have to understand; their understanding isn't what delivered them from the angel of death. Even their obedience isn't directly what saved them. Yes, God told them to do it and they would be saved, but that was the beginning lesson in the power and faithfulness of God. God was teaching them to act on what He told them He would be faithful to do. He wasn't telling Israel to buy His deliverance; God's deliverance was available to all who were willing to openly confess their trust in it and take it.

So, what was the confession God called on them to make? It was a confession in blood. It was a testimony, a plea. It was a bold, unapologetic, public confession of God's Lordship and faithfulness.

When a judge asks an accused person how he pleas, the accused doesn't answer with something that sounds like a question or a meek request. He answers boldly and clearly either "guilty" or "not guilty." He is making a claim of truth; committing to a statement of truth. And then he submits to the consequences of that claim.

Whether they knew it or not, the children of Israel were testifying. They were committing to a public statement of truth that Pharaoh was not god and the God of Moses was. They were making a plea about the power of God to deliver them. And God told them to make it with blood.

Our Testimony

What are we really doing when we plead the blood? We are making a statement we can't back out of. And we most often do it in desperation.

Desperation is what you're left with when you have nowhere else to turn.

Despair is what life ultimately comes to for those without Jesus—some just don't know it yet. The answer is to plead the blood of Jesus.

Despair is what many Christians end up feeling when they are slow to learn how to walk in daily dependence on God. Their unstable faith and dullness of hearing leads them to walls they can't get around. But they are free to plead the blood of Jesus over the despair and the walls and find renewed strength by trusting the Lord.

Desperate is what life was for Israel while they were in bondage in Egypt. Without even knowing it, they pleaded the blood of Jesus.

Sometimes we only remember to stand boldly on the trustworthiness of our God when we have no other option—when we run out of clever solutions. God loves it when we finally remember that living like people who are alive to God isn't about our cleverness or strength or knowledge or leadership abilities. Then, we remember it's about Him. It's about God's goodness, God's trustworthiness, God's power, and God's faithfulness to His word. God looks for the day when we remember and live by faith without desperation.

You can plead your faith in the blood of Jesus in everyday things. You do that by standing on the Word of God as a rock that can't be moved. You stand on the Word by speaking it into your life and the lives of others as the only foundation on which you stand. And when you speak the Word, you are actually pleading the Word. And the Word is Jesus Christ Himself (John 1:1).

But there is one aspect of such a confession or plea that must be present. Without it the plea is nothing but a lie. Again, a true plea is not something you change your mind about later. It isn't something you carry around like a key in your pocket until you need to unlock something. A plea is a statement your whole life is committed to—it's burning your bridges behind you. You take a stand, and that's it—no matter what.

But remember, the power of the blood of Jesus is in the blood itself. It's in the great victory over death Jesus won for us when He spilled His blood. We cannot add any power to the blood by pleading it in an eloquent way or with more intensity. But we will very quickly cut ourselves off from the power available through the blood by lying when we make our plea. We lie when our pleas don't square with the overall testimony of our lives.

Simon, the sorcerer, understood the power of

the blood of Jesus, and he wanted that power. He just didn't want Jesus, and we know what happened to him (Acts 8:18-21). Look it up and see what happens when someone wants the power of the blood without accepting the One to whom it belongs.

In James 1 we are taught that being double-minded robs us of the grace God desires to give us. Double-mindedness occurs when we have divided allegiance. For example, we are double-minded when we say we're trusting Jesus but then continue to live like we have no God by worrying about things and struggling to save ourselves. It contaminates our confession with untruth. We are saying great things but not living by them. God says He won't bless it because it isn't real faith.

> *But let him ask in faith, nothing wavering. For he that wavereth is like a wave of the sea driven with the wind and tossed. For let not that man think that he shall receive any thing of the Lord. A double minded man is unstable in all his ways.*
>
> ~JAMES 1:6-8

Don't water down your plea with doubt just because God's timing isn't your timing. Don't look for alternatives when your plea doesn't produce the exact results you're looking for. If you do, then it wasn't an honest plea. And you can't expect your plea in times of need to be given much power if the rest of your life pleads commitment to everything but the blood of Jesus!

The story about Vicki Winans' son, who had drifted in his walk with God, wasn't a case of God overlooking double-mindedness. Coconut wasn't double-minded at all. His whole life— what he said and how he lived—had cooled towards God. God used desperation to remind Coconut of what he had forgotten—that God is as near as our breath. When Coconut breathed out a plea of faith in the blood of Jesus, God showed Himself strong. Coconut's life was probably changed forever, wouldn't you think?

But if we respond to such grace from God with shallow devotion to Him until our next crisis, we may soon find our pleas going unanswered.

The bottom line is this—the power of the blood is more available to us the more we belong to Jesus. Underline these words: It isn't about "works;" it's about our testimony. If a plea is spoken on top of an overall lifestyle that says "Amen" to the plea, the plea becomes like a shout to the Lord. I believe God finds it irresistible!

We must be true to the blood of Jesus in all our confessions in life to see the full power of the blood brought to bear when we claim it.

Now let's look at another subject that relates to pleading the blood of Jesus—communion as a confession and a relationship.

⌐ SITTING TOGETHER ⌐

But God, who is rich in mercy, for his great love wherewith he loved us, Even when we were dead in sins, hath quickened us together with Christ, (by grace ye are saved;) And hath raised us up together, and made us sit together in heavenly places in Christ Jesus.

~ EPHESIANS 2:4-6

The main thing you should notice about the above verse is that Paul says God "hath" (past tense) raised us up and seated us together with

Christ Jesus in heavenly places. Spiritually, we are already raised and we already sit together with our Lord. But what does Paul mean by "sit together"? When people talk about sitting together, it almost always means one of two things: Either a committee meeting is going on or food and fellowship are being shared. Our life in Christ is both. As we worship Jesus and live in Him, we are meeting and eating with Him.

When we are on our knees, wrestling with Jesus over our marriage, our children, our work, our sins, our church or anything else, we are doing business with Him. We are bowing our knee to our Lord and meeting Him face to face in order to trade our cares for His promises. There's a kind of transaction going on each time we go to Him. But we are also sitting together with Him in loving fellowship as our Brother. We have more than a transaction with Jesus; we have a relationship. We sit at His feet to be taught and ruled by Him, but we also sit with Him at the Father's table to share the Father's blessings equally as family.

The power of Jesus and His blood is crucial

to our life and our faith. But we must always remember that Jesus suffered and died for far more than our rescue. He didn't suffer the cross and the loss of the innocent relationship He had with God just so we could clean up, march straight, and look good for Him. He saved us for Himself. He wants to have the same communion with us that He has with the Father.

> *Neither pray I for these alone, but for them also which shall believe on me through their word; That they all may be one; as thou, Father, art in me, and I in thee, that they also may be one in us: that the world may believe that thou hast sent me. And the glory which thou gavest me I have given them;* that they may be one, even as we are one.
>
> ~ *JOHN 17:20-22*; emphasis mine

Jesus prayed for us to be one with Him and with each other. While the children of Israel were safe behind their blood-stained doors from the angel of death, each family shared a special meal according to God's instructions. This meal became an annual feast known as Passover. It is special, not just because it is a time to remember how God delivered Israel from bondage and death (transaction); but it was a moment of communion with God (relationship). There was more than just obedience to a commanding God—there was real relationship. That first Passover was the first time since the fall of Adam that God was intimate with an entire people the way He always desired to be. God had gathered Israel safely under His wings and fellowshipped with them over a meal while they worshiped Him for His deliverance. That's what communion with God is.

Israel didn't understand the real significance of the meal, and they didn't know anything about the redemption the meal represented. They just shared it in faith, expecting God's promises to be fulfilled. More importantly, they didn't put faith in anything else.

⌐ THE POWER OF COMMUNION ¬

So "being one" is about intimate relationship or communion. And it is also about a faithful commitment to each other. It's not even about

"I'll stick with you if you stick with me." The kind of oneness Jesus was praying for is certain and unbreakable. He said it's like the oneness He has with His Father. And now He is saying to us, "I'm holding onto you, and I'm never letting go." If we want to have true communion with Jesus and power in our pleas, we must say the same thing to Him—and mean it.

But we're human, and sometimes our flesh is weak. One day we might think our trust in God is unshakable, but the next day we may have doubt about God's promises applying to us. We might have total confidence in the power of the blood of Jesus to work in a situation, but then we begin to lose confidence when there are setbacks. We may stand firm on the Word in the presence of fellow believers but, at the same time, we have a whole different agenda we're trusting in for our needs and plans.

None of these unstable ways are anything like real communion with Jesus. As I have already shown you, they are actually lies to God. We say out of one corner of our mouth, "Lord, You are my King, and I have no other. Your Word is true, and I will trust no other." Then out the other side of our mouths, we say, "If I don't get some money in time to keep from losing my car, I'm going to stop tithing," or "God must want me to suffer for some reason or else He'd answer my prayers for healing," or "I just don't have time to worship and pray and study God's word." We'd never say anything like this if Jesus were standing right beside us in the flesh, would we?

But the fact is He has already promised that He is with us every moment and He will never leave us. He's holding onto us and never letting go. How can we lie to Jesus the way we do? How can we plead the blood of Jesus as though we are holding onto Him as tightly as He is holding onto us, but then turn our backs on Him with words or attitudes of doubt and ingratitude? How can we speak the Word to someone in need of encouragement as though we speak it continually to ourselves, but then we repeat the faithless things Satan whispers in our ears? People, let's stop lying to Jesus.

Communion is also what we call that part of our worship when we take bread and wine.

Unfortunately, this part of worship has faded in most churches to rare use and casual understanding. It is more than stale liturgy or a ceremony of remembrance; it is a way we truly sit down together as a body with Jesus to share our relationship with Him; it is a moment in which we can take part in the tenderness of a loving embrace with Jesus and also the firmness of a plea about who Jesus is and who we are in Him; it is a time He told us to treasure and share together often because, when we do, we bless Him and ourselves.

Communion means to be one, and when we share the bread and wine (or grape juice) at the meal we call "communion," one of the many things we are doing is drawing near to Jesus. We are embracing our oneness with Him. But many don't recognize that we are also embracing each other. When we take the bread in communion, we recognize it as the body of Christ. But we must remember that, as Jesus dwells within us, we are the body of Christ. So in communion, we not only make a plea of receiving Jesus, we receive all of our brothers and sisters, who are each a part of the body of Christ. We are one with Jesus and with each other when we realize we are one body. If we will remember this, every time we celebrate communion we will build greater unity, love, and power within the body. So taking the bread and wine of communion is a plea. It is a testimony that says we trust only in the spilled blood and broken body of Jesus to save us and give us life.

⌐ BEING TRUE TO THE BLOOD ¬

Tragically, there are many who are not true to their plea. Instead of flourishing in the abundant life available to them, many brothers and sisters indulge in lesser, even damaging, things as ways to cope with life. Paul would say they are taking communion in an unworthy manner (1 Corinthians 11:27-31). They're basically lying to God because they don't live by the faith they claim in their communion plea. How can God bless it?

There is nothing more distasteful to God than when a proud and loud confession of faith is used to hide a heart full of unbelief. It is better to struggle honestly and openly with sin and unbelief before God and the body of Christ and accept forgiveness than to make a lying plea. Be true to the blood of Jesus in your heart first. A life of victory that pleases God will grow out of a faithful and honest heart.

> *For the eyes of the LORD run to and fro throughout the whole earth, to shew himself strong in the behalf of them whose heart is perfect toward him.*
>
> ~ 2 CHRONICLES 16:9

⌐ THE HOUND OF HEAVEN ⌐

The poet Francis Thompson wrote a long poem that's a little difficult to read and even harder to understand. But even with little understanding it's easy to be moved by it. In the 182 lines of *The Hound of Heaven*, Thompson describes what it is like to spend one's life trying to escape the stubborn, pursuing love of God. The poem begins with these lines:

> *I fled Him, down the nights and down the days;*
> *I fled Him, down the arches of the years;*

I fled Him, down the labyrinthine ways
Of my own mind; and in the mist of tears
I hid from Him, and under running laughter.
Up vistaed hopes I sped;
And shot, precipitated,
Adown Titanic glooms of chasmed fears,
From those strong Feet that followed, followed after.

His commitment to run away sounds almost like panic and fear. And the running continues through pages of verse describing the dreadful anguish of trying to escape a pursuer's obsession. Eventually, the runner is weary and loses hope of finding the peace he is seeking. He tires from a life of running and surrenders to inevitable capture by what he believes is a vicious hunter.

But instead of the imagined harm he had come to expect from a painful life of running, a voice of tenderness came to him. It said nothing that was taken from him in life was meant for harm, but so that he might seek those things in the one who pursued him. Finally, he understood the pursuer's heart, as the pursuer spoke these last lines:

"Ah, fondest, blindest, weakest,
I am He Whom thou seekest!
Thou dravest love from thee, who dravest me."

As I said at the beginning of this book, God made us to know Him. He put a hunger within each of us that only He can fulfill. But we are hard-headed and self-centered. Until we are forced to turn and face the love of God, we try to fulfill all our hunger with mere distractions offered by the world. When we drive God's love away, we lose the only pure love available to us.

He loves us more deeply and widely and highly than we can possibly know. In fact, it must be very painful for God when men try to drive away the very One they unknowingly long for. But we cannot exhaust God's will! We can't wear Him out!

Jesus said all whom the Father has given to Him will come to Him (John 6:37), and it killed Jesus to make sure that happens. The frighteningly beautiful truth is that He is willing for it to almost kill us too—just for Him to win our hearts.

When we finally stop trying to save ourselves—when we stop trying to make our lives work without God and we allow our hearts to be captured—that's just the beginning.

He wants it all. He wants everything we are. He wants us to hold nothing back. He wants our fears, our pain, our self-hatred, our sin, our whole past, present, and future.

Forget the past! Stop fearing the future! Humble trust in the value of the blood of Jesus makes that possible. And when you allow Jesus to discard your past, you will be able and responsible to do the same for others.

If God forgives so much from us who were condemned to death, how dare we not forgive those who offend us? We are not named by what we've done or by what is done to us. We are ultimately named by whose we are.

If Jesus is yours and you are His, your name is Beloved. Be true to the blood of Jesus, brothers and sisters. Be true to the blood and be restored.

If you don't know Jesus Christ as your personal Lord and Savior, you are encouraged to make this decision today as you pray the following prayer:

Heavenly Father, I recognize and admit that I am a sinner.

I turn from my sins, confess with my mouth, and believe in my heart that Jesus is Lord.

I believe that He lived, died, and was raised from the dead for my salvation.

I receive my salvation and all of its benefits right now.

Lord, thank You for saving me this day.

In Jesus' name, I pray.

Amen!

To learn more about Paula White Ministries,
please write to:

Paula White Ministries
PO Box 25151
Tampa FL 33622

Or call the Prayer Line at 813-874-7729

Visit the website at www.paulawhite.org

Product order line: 800-992-8892